THE WORLD OF ROBOTS

BATTLING FOR VICTORY
THE COOLEST ROBOT COMPETITIONS

BY KATHRYN CLAY

Consultant:
Barbara J. Fox
Professor Emerita
North Carolina State University

CAPSTONE PRESS
a capstone imprint

Blazers Books are published by Capstone Press,
1710 Roe Crest Drive, North Mankato, Minnesota 56003
www.capstonepub.com

Library of Congress Cataloging-in-Publication Data
Clay, Kathryn, author.
Battling for victory : the coolest robot competitions / by Kathryn Clay.
pages cm.—(Blazers books. The world of robots)
Audience: Ages 8–13.
Audience: Grades 4 to 6.
Summary: "Describes various competitions and games involving
robots"—Provided by publisher.
Includes bibliographical references and index.
ISBN 978-1-4765-3974-4 (library binding)
ISBN 978-1-4765-5114-2 (paperback)
ISBN 978-1-4765-5955-1 (ebook PDF)
1. Mobile robots—Competitions—Juvenile literature. 2. Robots—Design and
construction—Juvenile literature. 3. Robotics—Juvenile literature. I. Title.
TJ211.415.C53 2014
629.8'932079—dc23   2013026492

Editorial Credits
Aaron Sautter, editor; Ted Williams, designer; Eric Gohl, media researcher;
Eric Manske, production specialist

Photo Credits
DARPA: 21; NASA: JPL-Caltech, 19; Newscom: EPA/Ingo Wagner, cover (bottom
left), Feature Photo Service, 14, Getty Images/AFP/Joyce Van Belkom, 7, Getty
Images/AFP/Robyn Beck, 13, imago sportfotodienst, 29, WENN/ZOB/JP5,
cover (bottom right), ZUMA Press/John Gastaldo, 22, ZUMA Press/Xu Liang,
17; RoboGames: Dave Schumaker, 4, 16, Rick Washburn Photography, 11, Sam
Coniglio, 8; Shutterstock: Ivan Nikulin, cover (top); Stefan Hrabar: CSIRO, 25, 26

Printed in the United States of America in Stevens Point, Wisconsin.
092013   007768WZS14

TABLE OF
CONTENTS

READY TO RUMBLE! 5

GOING FOR THE GOLD 6

SMASH ... CRASH ... CRUNCH! . . 12

CHAMPIONSHIP CHALLENGES . . . 18

BUILDING THE FUTURE 28

GLOSSARY 30

READ MORE 31

INTERNET SITES 31

INDEX 32

ROBOT FACT

Robots compete in many different events held around the world.

READY TO RUMBLE!

Crunch! Sparks fly as two **robots** clash in the ring. Fierce **competitions** match one robot against another. Only the smartest and toughest robot will win.

robot—a machine programmed to do jobs usually performed by a person

competition—a contest

Going for the Gold

Robots from around the world compete in the Robocup soccer tournament. Robots in the **humanoid** league walk, run, and kick like people do.

humanoid—a robot that has a human form

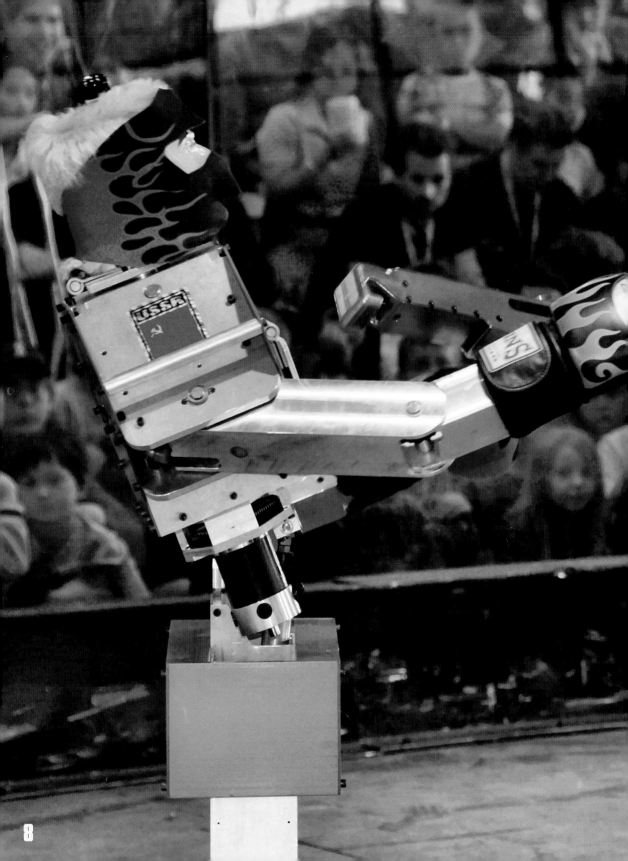

ROBOGAMES

Robots compete in more than 50 events at the RoboGames. Competitions include weightlifting, boxing, and street hockey.

ROBOT FACT

Mech Warfare is a popular RoboGames event. Robots attack each other with flamethrowers, rockets, and other weapons. The last robot standing wins.

ROBOT MUSICIANS

Not all RoboGames are rough and tough. The ArtBot-Musical competition features robots that play music on their own. These robots play pianos, drums, or homemade instruments.

SMASH ... CRASH... CRUNCH!

BATTLEBOTS

Look to BattleBots for thrilling robot action! The BattleBox is full of spinning saw blades and sharp floor spikes. During each BotBout match, two robots bump, crash, and push each other into the **obstacles**.

obstacle—something that gets in the way or blocks progress

ROBOT FACT
Winner-take-all robot battles started with Critter Crunch in 1989. The winner beat other robots by shooting a can of Silly String.

ROBOT FACT

BattleBot losers compete in the Robot Rumble. Each robot tries to disable as many robots as it can in five minutes.

BATTLEBOT TEAMS

BattleBot teams are split into three **divisions**—professional, college, and high school. Each team's robot fights for three minutes, or until one can't move. Eventually, one team in each division becomes the champion.

division—a group of people or teams in a certain category for a competition

ROBOT WRESTLERS

Sumo wrestling robots face off in round rings. Each robot tries to push the other out of the ring. The first robot to win two out of three times wins the match.

CHAMPIONSHIP CHALLENGES

FIRST COMPETITIONS

High school students can compete in the For Inspiration and Recognition of Science and Technology (FIRST) competition. This contest features **autonomous** robots that complete different tasks on their own.

autonomous—able to control oneself; autonomous robots are not operated by a person

ROBOT FACT

In 2013 the theme of the FIRST competition was Ultimate Ascent. Teams used robots to toss flying discs into a goal.

DARPA ROBOTICS CHALLENGE (DRC)

The DRC is put on by the U.S. Department of Defense. Designers compete to build robots that can help in emergencies and disasters. The DARPA competition offers a $2 million prize.

DARPA scientists are designing rescue robots to work in dangerous areas after earthquakes and other disasters.

ROBOT FACT

In 2004 and 2005, teams competed in the DARPA Grand Challenge. It featured robotic cars that drove themselves in an off-road race.

ROBOSUB

The RoboSub contest takes place in San Diego, California. Teams of high school and college students build robots that travel underwater. The robots go through obstacle courses and fire **torpedoes**.

ROBOT FACT

Younger students compete by building SeaPerch robots to explore underwater.

torpedo—an underwater missile

UAV CHALLENGE-OUTBACK RESCUE

The **UAV** Challenge-**Outback** Rescue features two competitions. The first part is the Airborne Delivery Challenge. Robotic planes drop emergency packages as close to a **mannequin** as possible.

UAV—unmanned aerial vehicle

outback—the flat desert areas of Australia; few people live in the outback

mannequin—a life-sized model of a human

ROBOT FACT

The mannequin used in the Outback Rescue challenge is nicknamed "Outback Joe."

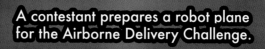

A contestant prepares a robot plane for the Airborne Delivery Challenge.

Outback Joe waits to be found somewhere in Australia.

The second part of Outback Rescue is the Search and Rescue Challenge. Robotic planes first search for Outback Joe in the countryside. After finding him, planes drop a rescue package nearby.

Building the Future

Competitions often lead to big improvements. Robots that explore oceans and help save people were developed from contests. The next incredible robot might be the one you help invent!

ROBOT FACT

Scientists hope robots can compete and win against human players in soccer's World Cup by 2050.

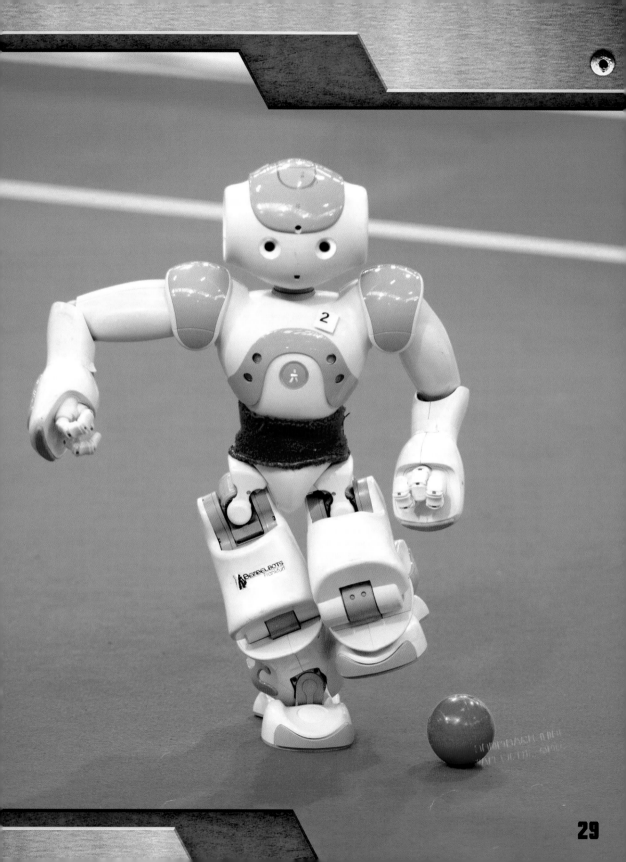

GLOSSARY

ascent (uh-SENT)—the process of moving upward

autonomous (aw-TAH-nuh-muhss)—able to control oneself; autonomous robots are not operated by a person

competition (kahm-puh-TI-shuhn)—a contest

division (duh-VI-shuhn)—a group of people or teams in a certain category for a competition

humanoid (HYOO-muh-noyd)—a robot that has a human form

mannequin (MAN-i-kin)—a life-sized model of a human

obstacle (OB-stuh-kuhl)—something that gets in the way or blocks progress

outback (OUT-back)—the flat desert areas of Australia; few people live in the outback

robot (ROH-bot)—a machine programmed to do jobs usually performed by a person

torpedo (tor-PEE-doh)—an underwater missile

UAV (YOO AY VEE)—unmanned aerial vehicle

READ MORE

Davis, Barbara J. *The Kids' Guide to Robots*. Kids' Guides. Mankato, Minn.: Capstone Press, 2010.

Oxlade, Chris. *Robots*. Explorers. New York: Kingfisher, 2013.

Stewart, Melissa. *Robots*. National Geographic Readers. Washington, D.C.: National Geographic, 2014.

INTERNET SITES

FactHound offers a safe, fun way to find Internet sites related to this book. All of the sites on FactHound have been researched by our staff.

Here's all you do:

Visit *www.facthound.com*

Type in this code: 9781476539744

Super-cool stuff! Check out projects, games and lots more at www.capstonekids.com

INDEX

ArtBot-Musical competition, 10

BattleBots, 12, 14, 15
BotBout matches, 12
boxing, 9

Critter Crunch, 12

DARPA Grand Challenge, 21
DARPA Robotics Challenge, 20

exploring oceans, 28

FIRST competitions, 18, 19

hockey, 9

Mech Warfare, 9

playing music, 10

Robocup, 6
RoboGames, 9, 10
RoboSub, 23
Robot Rumble, 14

saving people, 28
SeaPerches, 23
soccer, 6, 28

UAV Challenge-Outback Rescue
    Airborne Delivery Challenge, 24
    Search and Rescue Challenge, 27

weightlifting, 9
wrestling, 16